It's Time for

Preschool

For More Booklets...

Interested in more copies of *It's Time for Preschool* to share with others? Each of the booklets in the *Me, Too!* series is available in packages of five.

Looking for guidance on every aspect of developing inclusive preschool strategies? The complete set of all six booklets in the *Me, Too!* series will provide you with extensive techniques for enhancing children's early years.

Contact Brookes Publishing Co. at *410-337-9580* or *1-800-638-3775*, or visit our web site at *www.brookespublishing.com.*

To write to the publisher: Paul H. Brookes Publishing Co., Post Office Box 10624, Baltimore, Maryland 21285-0624, U.S.A.

Typeset by Integrated Publishing Solutions, Grand Rapids, Michigan.
Manufactured in the United States of America by H & N Printing & Graphics, Timonium, Maryland.
Cover art and interior illustrations by Lori Esposito.

The *Me, Too!* series is based on research conducted through the Early Childhood Research Institute on Inclusion supported by Grant #HO242K4004 from the U.S. Department of Education, Office of Special Education Programs. No official endorsement by the federal government should be inferred.

Parent quotes and case scenarios are from actual people and events. In all instances, names have been changed; in some instances, identifying details have been altered to protect confidentiality.

Library of Congress Cataloging-in-Publication Data

It's time for preschool / [Marci J. Hanson... et al.]
p. cm.— (Me, too!)
ISBN 1-55766-510-9
1. School choice—United States—Handbooks, manuals, etc. 2. Nursery schools—United States—Evaluation—Handbooks, manuals, etc. 3. Handicapped children—Education—United States—Handbooks, manuals, etc.
I. Hanson, Marci J. II. Series.
LB1027.9 .I88 2001
372.21′6—dc21

00-068934

British Library Cataloguing in Publication data are available from the British Library.

Baltimore • London • Toronto • Sydney

Introduction

Chances are, if you're reading this booklet, you have a child between the ages of 2 and 5 years. It's a time of new experiences and challenges for children and their parents. As a parent, you are accustomed to making decisions to help your child grow, develop, and learn in appropriate ways, but now, you will also be deciding how to help your child belong and participate in school and other community activities. Will your child make friends? Will your child know how to behave? Will your child be able to do the things the other children are doing?

This booklet is one in a series called *Me, Too!*, designed particularly for families of young children with disabilities. Although these booklets are written directly to parents and other family members, teachers, child care providers, and other professionals will find them valuable, too. Plan to pass these booklets back and forth among the adults who are important in your child's life. Here is a brief description of each booklet:

Introducing Me: This booklet is different from the other booklets because it is one that you create. You fill out the pages to tell others about your child. Share this booklet with your child's teachers and with the other professionals and caregivers who work with your child.

It's Time for Preschool: This booklet helps you learn more about selecting a preschool for your child, connecting with teachers and other families, knowing what the law guarantees you, and making the early school years a positive experience for your child.

My Community, My Family: This booklet helps you learn about building good relationships between your family and others in the community. You will find good advice on locating appropriate, accessible programs and activities. Strategies also are included for making activities meet the needs of all children.

My New Friends: This booklet explores ways that you can encourage friendships between children. The importance of friendships is highlighted through suggestions designed to help your child develop friendships with classmates and make new friends in the community.

On My Best Behavior: This booklet will help you understand your child's behavior. You will learn techniques to help you support positive behavior, discourage negative behavior, and avoid behavior problems by planning ahead for new situations.

Look What I Can Do Now: This booklet focuses on introducing strategies for modifying schedules and the physical environment to make it easier for your child to participate in programs and activities.

In each of these booklets, we will be talking about the term *inclusion*. Inclusion usually refers to the joint participation of children with and without disabilities in school and community programs and in activities. Although people may think of inclusion as something that only happens at school, inclusion is actually a very broad concept that refers to participation in many settings (e.g., child care, recreational programs, libraries, religious activities, athletic organizations, museums). In the most general sense, inclusion is about belonging. When a child belongs, he or she is a part of a group and has opportunities to join activities with other children. Inclusion is good for children.

We hope that the *Me, Too!* series will help you as you begin to develop inclusive strategies to meet your family's needs. You will find experiences and recommendations that other parents have shared with us to help you. We address issues and decisions commonly faced by parents and suggest strategies for you to consider when planning for your child and family. As you study these ideas, always keep in mind that you, as a parent, are the expert as to what works for your family!

It's Time for Preschool

It's natural for parents to be excited and apprehensive about their child's first day of school. You aren't alone if you find yourself asking, "Will my child like school? Will my child be safe? Will teachers understand my child's needs? Will my child make friends?" Feelings of uneasiness are understandable, and it's often helpful to talk with parents, teachers, therapists, physicians, school administrators, members of family support groups, and others who have had similar experiences.

This booklet helps you anticipate what is ahead as you make plans for your child's first school experience. You will want to think about what is important to you in a program, develop a plan of action to find the right one for your child, and have a back-up plan in mind. The more you know as a parent, the more prepared you will be to choose the most appropriate options for your child. Look for the paintbrush icon for special tips.

CHOOSING A PRESCHOOL PROGRAM

The best way to learn what different programs have to offer is to visit them, but first, prepare yourself. Take some time to think about your expectations and what you want for your child, then be sure to talk to others.

Preparing to Visit

Thinking about programs in terms of how they will benefit your child is a good way to start. You may want to consider the amount of exposure to other children that your child will have, the play opportunities offered by the program's schedule, and the overall environment. Does the program schedule time to develop communication skills or help children learn English as a second language? Will the program help your child prepare for grade school by nurturing skills such as following directions, listening, and working in groups? Most parents choose programs that will provide their children with opportunities to play and socialize. It is through these activities that young children learn. Some parents look for structured learning environments and routines that emphasize preacademics—learning letters, numbers, and reading. You might also want to think about whether a program reinforces skills that you teach your child at home. Programs designed for groups of young children can be great places for your child to continue learning social skills such as sharing, taking turns, and using good manners, as well as self-help skills such as feeding, dressing, and toileting.

Before you begin to visit programs, you can enlist the help of friends, neighbors, and others in your community. Don't be reluctant to seek information. After all, your child has the right to have all of his educational needs met. For information about programs,

✔ *Ask your friends who have young children or ask other parents you meet at parent groups for suggestions and recommendations about programs and activities.*

✔ *Check with local schools to see if they have lists of preschool programs in the community.*

Look into programs previously attended by other children or family members.

You also will want to ask therapists, physicians, social workers, and other care providers to suggest good programs and activities for your child. Get the conversation going by asking questions such as the following:

- What programs do you recommend for my child?
- Why do you recommend these programs?
- How would these programs benefit my child?
- Will my child need special equipment or specific adaptations to fully participate in the program activities?
- Do you know anyone else I can talk to about different program options?

Talking to professionals who know your child can help you find possible matches for your family. They may offer other advice or make suggestions about what to look for in the programs you will visit. Programs—including Head Start programs, parent cooperatives, community and religious preschools, child care centers or family child care programs, school district preschool programs, child development centers, and recreational programs—may be available in a number of settings.

If you can, visit programs when other children are present. See whether children with and without disabilities learn and participate together and enjoy opportunities to play with each other throughout the day. You will also be able to make sure that you are comfortable with the way the program staff members administer therapies and special education services. Let's look more specifically at what you will want to observe.

Visiting Programs

As you visit programs, ask yourself the following questions to help decide which program is best for your child:

- Can I imagine my child in this environment?
- Do the children in the program seem happy?
- What do I like and dislike about the teacher?
- What do I like and dislike about how the teacher interacts with the children?
- Would my child enjoy participating in the activities at this program?
- Would my child enjoy being with the adults and other children in this program?
- What do I like and dislike about the physical space in the classroom and in the outdoor area? What adaptations or changes would be needed for my child to participate in activities?
- Are the staff members interested in knowing more about my child and our family?
- What information will I share, and how will I share it?
- Are the staff members respectful of our family's cultural beliefs, language, and values?
- How do my goals for my child match the program's goals?

Be sure that you talk with the program director or some of the teachers and staff members while you are visiting. This is one of the best ways to learn about specific programs. Start by asking them a few questions that will help you determine how well a program will fit your child's needs:

- What is the mission statement or philosophy of your program?
- Can you tell me about your curriculum and what you think is important for children to learn?
- How do you think young children learn best?
- Can you tell me about your classroom?

- What are your methods of child behavior management?
- How do you communicate with families?
- What resources and supports are available to families in your program?
- Do you provide regular training for teachers and parents?
- What is your professional background and experience?

Of course, as you are visiting, you will want to be thinking about other questions as well. Are staff members qualified and trained? Do they follow safety, health, and hygiene procedures? Does the program fit your family's schedule? For some parents, it will be important for child care to be available before and after work hours and for the program to be in a convenient location. You may also want to find out if the program plans ahead to help prepare children for their future school settings. Such plans are often called *transition plans*. Ask, too, about meetings for parents. Programs for which staff members organize meetings with families, parent groups, and members of professional organizations are more likely to be concerned about meeting the individual needs of children.

The National Association for the Education of Young Children (NAEYC, 2000) provides 10 general guidelines that reflect good programs for all young children in the brochure titled *Choosing a Good Early Childhood Program: Questions and Answers*. Generally, a preschool program is good if

- Children spend most of their time working with materials and playing with other children.
- Children have access to various activities throughout the day.
- Teachers work with individual children, small groups, and the whole group at different times during the day.
- The classroom is decorated with children's original artwork, their own writing, and stories that they have dictated.

- Children learn within meaningful contexts.
- Children work on projects and have periods of time to play and explore.
- Children have an opportunity to play outside every day.
- Teachers read books to children individually or in small groups throughout the day.
- The curriculum is adapted for those who are ahead as well as for those who need additional help.
- Children and their families feel safe and secure within their early childhood program.

Identifying Differences Among Programs

As you are weighing the strengths and weaknesses of the programs that you visit based on these questions and guidelines, you also will want to learn more about the specific characteristics of each program:

- *Schedule:* Preschools are held for half days, for full days, or for variable hours and may or may not include after-school care options.

- *Cost:* The costs of programs range from no cost to costs assessed on sliding scales to full payment of fees by families.
- *Eligibility requirements:* Special requirements that must be met in order for a child to attend may include the proximity of her home to the program, family income, languages spoken, and whether the child is toilet trained or able to walk independently.
- *Parent involvement:* In some programs, parents are asked to work in the classroom or to help with other activities; other programs schedule parent group meetings.
- *Support:* Some programs provide consultants and resource personnel in the areas of mental health, speech-language therapy, occupational therapy, or physical therapy.
- *Teaching arrangement:* Teachers work together using a variety of models, and programs include children with disabilities in different ways. The many factors influencing the decisions of program staff members include the kind of program it is, available opportunities in the community, and available resources (e.g., time, money, staff). Preschool and child care programs use several common models to include children with disabilities:
    - *Itinerant teaching model:* Children with and without disabilities learn in the same environment. Special education teachers and therapists visit the program to provide various support services.
    - *Team teaching model:* An early childhood teacher and a special education teacher work as a team in the classroom. Related services—such as physical therapy or speech-language therapy—usually are provided in the same setting.
    - *Early childhood teaching model:* An early childhood teacher works with all of the children, regardless of whether they have special needs. There is little contact with special education teachers.

  - *Special education teaching model:* A special education teacher is responsible for a majority of classroom activities. There is less contact with general early childhood teachers. In this model, typically developing children often serve as peer models or helpers for children with disabilities.
  - *Integrated activities model:* Children with disabilities and typically developing children participate in joint activities for a portion of the day but spend most of their day in separate classes. Special education and related services typically are provided in a separate classroom.
- *Philosophy:* Some programs emphasize play or preacademics; other programs emphasize learning about others.
- *Curriculum:* Teachers use the term *curriculum* to describe their plans for teaching children and arranging the classroom. A curriculum is a prepared plan of what and how to teach. It describes the methods that teachers use to organize the space and materials in the classroom, manage class time, and interact with the children. The curriculum for your child will include goals for the whole group, as well as goals that address your child's needs. As teachers and special support staff members make adaptations to help children participate and learn, these adaptations are reflected in their curriculum plan.

Every program will have its own unique characteristics, and you will find that the many differences among programs will be primary factors in your decision-making process. As you move forward in your evaluation, your understanding of the special education process will deepen. You will want to learn more about your child's rights to an inclusive education.

KNOWING YOUR CHILD'S RIGHTS

Before we talk about rights, it's important to remind ourselves, and those around us, that a child's right to receive a free and ap-

propriate public education (FAPE) isn't just about a legal requirement. Inclusion of children with disabilities is important for a number of reasons:

- *It's fair.* Most young children spend a certain amount of their time in preschools, in child care centers, and participating in community activities. From an ethical perspective, children with disabilities deserve these opportunities as well.
- *It's good for children.* When children spend time with others from diverse backgrounds and ability levels, they learn about cooperation and differences. Children with disabilities are often more motivated to do new things if they have models to imitate. Peers encourage many aspects of early development, such as language and social skills.
- *It's the law.* Certain laws, such as the Individuals with Disabilities Education Act (IDEA) and the Americans with Disabilities Act (ADA), prevent discrimination against people with disabilities and ensure that everyone has access to public services, including education.

In the introduction to this booklet, we explained the term *inclusion.* Although inclusion isn't specifically defined in the federal legislation, it is commonly used to describe the joint participation of children with and without disabilities in school and community programs and in activities. Terms expressing the same general idea that you might have heard in previous years include *integration* or *mainstreaming.* You will want to familiarize yourself with some of the other terms and acronyms that you are likely to hear, and we introduce some in the following section. Don't forget that it is always appropriate to ask someone who uses a term that you don't recognize to explain what he or she means. Let's look more specifically at some of the guarantees that you and your child receive according to federal law.

The Federal Laws

Knowing as much as you can about disability, special education, and access laws will make it easier for you to advocate for your child. Several laws affect young children and their families.

Americans with Disabilities Act (ADA) The ADA, enacted in 1990, ensures the full civil rights of individuals with disabilities. The ADA also guarantees equal opportunities for people with disabilities in terms of employment, transportation, telecommunications, state and local government services, and public accommodation. Public accommodation, which includes child care programs and family child care homes, must make reasonable modifications in policies and procedures to accommodate children and adults with disabilities.

Individuals with Disabilities Education Act (IDEA) IDEA ensures that children who are eligible for special education receive a free and appropriate public education (FAPE) in the least restrictive environment (LRE), that is, an environment in which learners with disabilities can succeed that is most similar to that of their peers. IDEA was named the Education for All Handicapped Children Act when it was first enacted in 1975, and you may still hear it referred to by this title or its original public law number, PL 94-142. It has since been amended and reauthorized several times. Mandated education services were extended to young children in 1986 under one of these revisions (PL 99-457). According to the latest amendments in 1997 (PL 105-17), provisions of IDEA include

- An *individualized family service plan (IFSP)* for children from birth to 3 years of age prepared by a team including parents: Parent involvement is an important part of the decision-making process. The IFSP is designed to coordinate services for infants and toddlers with special needs. Under Part C (formerly Part H) of IDEA, young children who exhibit developmental delay, are at risk for developmental delay, or have been diagnosed with a condition that is likely to result in developmental delay are eligible for early intervention services that are coordinated through the creation of an IFSP. The extent of these services and the criteria for eligibility may differ slightly from state to state, but all states are provided with incentives under IDEA's Part C to offer early intervention for children from birth to 3 years of age.

- An *individualized education program (IEP)* for children from ages 3 to 5 years prepared by an educational team: As with the IFSP, the parent, as a member of the team, is able to work closely with the team's other members to determine which educational strategies and intervention options are best for the child. Teams typically include a general educator, a special educator, a psychologist, and other related specialists (e.g., medical personnel, a physical therapist, a speech-language pathologist). Beginning with a child's third birthday, an IEP is prepared each year that a child is in school. Part B of IDEA refers to services for children between ages 3 and 5 years.

- *Related services* that are necessary to the educational needs of the child: These could include speech-language therapy, occupational therapy, physical therapy, nutritional services, and so forth.

- *Nondiscriminatory testing* to assess young children's development in a manner that is appropriate to their disability and cultural and linguistic background: This requires the informed consent of the parent.

- *Procedural safeguards* that include a means of resolving disputes and ensuring that children's and parents' rights are realized: This is known as *due process*.

If you have not already established an IFSP or an IEP and have questions concerning your child, talk to your child's pediatrician or a local preschool administrator. The members of your child's IFSP or IEP team may be able to suggest different programs to meet your child's and family's needs.

Section 504 of the Rehabilitation Act Section 504 of the Rehabilitation Act, which was originally enacted in 1973 and since amended and reauthorized, prohibits discrimination against individuals with disabilities by any establishment that receives federal funds.

Technology-Related Assistance for Individuals with Disabilities Act Known as the *Tech Act*, this federal law, enacted in 1988, provides for assistive technology, or any "tool or item that increases, maintains, and improves functional capabilities of individuals with disabilities," to be part of your child's IEP. It also allocates federal funds for helping states develop easily available, consumer-responsive systems of access to assistive technology, technology services, and information.

There are many ways to get information about the laws that can assist you in ensuring that your child is able to participate in the educational opportunities to which he or she is entitled. Contacting family resource and training centers or talking with families who have experience with special education and legal systems are good ways to start. You can also consult legal and advocacy groups and local state and education agencies that may publish handbooks about special education laws. Consider visiting the government documents section of your local library, or search the Internet for related web sites (free access is available at many public libraries) for additional information about special education and the law.

If the material you find seems confusing, try talking with other families or advocacy groups who already are familiar with the laws. Advocacy groups sometimes sponsor seminars that can help get you up to speed on the IFSP and IEP process. These programs often plan segments that summarize and explain laws related to special education and access. Once you understand the information, you can help other families and children with disabilities by sharing your knowledge. Discuss the main points of different laws, share handouts and summary sheets that you have found useful, and let others in your community know about books, organizations, and web sites that you would recommend. Remember, you will need to be aware of changes over the years and keep up with current special education legal issues.

MAKING SURE INCLUSION IS A GOOD EXPERIENCE FOR YOUR CHILD

Once you understand your child's rights and have found a preschool that meets her needs, you may find that you are looking for other ways of providing support that will help make inclusion a positive experience. Asking people already familiar with your child to help new teachers, students, and activity leaders get to know your child is one type of support that helps ease transitions. An important transition occurs when children are about to begin preschool. Soon after your child's second birthday or no later than 3 months before preschool begins, the IFSP team should begin designing a transition plan to prepare for preschool and the IEP. According to federal legislation, the family should be a part of the planning process, and the program must include a policy that describes how families will be included in the transition process. Furthermore, the transition plan should include important contacts, information about further assessments or testing, a description of proposed therapy services, an outline of the IEP schedule, a review of individual and family rights, and a record of plans for preparing and developing the IEP.

In a more general sense, though, transition refers to any time your child changes from one program or activity to the next. It is wise to plan for these changes. The following ideas may help you plan ahead to make transitions easier for your child:

Try to take your child to visit a new program several times before the first day. Visit on a weekend or during the evening when other children are not present. Give your child a chance to explore the room at his own pace and without distractions. Visit again during class so that your child knows what it will be like with other children present.

Ask whether you or another relative can be there for support during those first few days. Explain that the company of someone with whom your child is comfortable can help him begin participating in program routines. Find out whether your child can bring a favorite familiar toy to ease the transition to the new program or setting.

Use a team approach to plan for your child's transition. Ask everyone—teachers, administrators, therapists, and others who work with and know your child—to join you in planning for your child's transition.

Laying the groundwork for smooth transitions is an excellent way to support your child, but sometimes, even when you have done all that you can to prepare your child, going to a new place where there are unfamiliar people or moving from activity to activity in the classroom can be difficult. Some children react to change by becoming angry and throwing tantrums; others become shy and withdraw from the group.

In certain situations, you may have to take special measures to change negative behavior, and other adults who know your child can offer great support.

Decide how you will prepare your child for changes and what kind of support you and others will give your child as changes occur. For example, plan to visit a new program ahead of time, and get to know your child's teachers before the school year begins. Also, arrange for the teacher to meet and spend some time with your child before the first day of school, or if your child is getting a new teacher or therapist, rehearse what to say and do when they meet. Stay informed about changes at your child's program, and work with the program staff members to support your child through transition. *On My Best Behavior* describes a variety of strategies to support your child in managing his behavior in new situations.

In addition to preparing your child and supporting her through transitions, you may have to help teachers and program staff members prepare for your child. Think about the most important things that others should know about your child, and share that information. Words, gestures, and signs that your child uses and understands; what your child does when angry or sad; what to do to help calm your child; and information about your child's special equipment or materials can be helpful to people just getting to know your child. One way to help others get to know and understand your child is to use the *Introducing Me* booklet to organize important information about your child's favorite activities, ways of communicating, and skills or talents. Some parents also make videos of their children on a family vacation or at birthday parties to help introduce their child to others.

Once staff members, teachers, parents, and other children know your child, try to strengthen the relationships you have with these individuals. Good relationships with service providers, program staff members, and other parents are important. Connecting with each other on a personal level will make it easier for you to trust one another, work together, and rely on each other for advice. In addition, be aware of ways to encourage friendships between your child and classmates. We all know that good friendships are an integral part of growing up, and when children are friends they also provide good models for each other and help each other learn. *My New Friends* provides detailed information about cultivating your child's school friendships and suggests that you look to community activities as well. In *My Community, My Family*, you can familiarize yourself with strategies for locating, planning, and making time for community activities that your child will enjoy.

Sometimes, even in inclusive activities and programs, you may have to make special changes to help your child participate. For instance, you may want to visit the program to determine which kinds of changes you could make to the furniture arrangement. Other situations may not require any physical adaptations, but you might notice that changing the schedule of events enables your child to participate in all activities. If it is difficult for your child to move quickly from one activity to the next,

The booklet *Look What I Can Do Now* is a good resource for ideas about adaptations that you and your child's teachers can make to ensure the participation of all children.

propose schedule changes so activities occurring in the same area also chronologically follow each other, or suggest "stretch time" between activities for children who need movement or physical activities to signal the transition from one activity to the next.

MEETING CHILDREN'S NEEDS

The advantages of good inclusive programs are not restricted to children with special needs. The instructional techniques used by special education teachers can be helpful to all children, and resources provided for children with disabilities often benefit typically developing children as well.

> "*I feel that even though my son is not entitled to any of those special services, there are people there that are going to be more aware of things.*"
>
> —Bernardo's father

In addition to the educational benefits of inclusive programs, children also learn about differences. Many parents believe that being around children with special needs helps their children learn to appreciate differences. As children learn to appreciate differences, they learn to be more accepting. For this reason, parents of children from many backgrounds with many ability levels seek inclusive programs.

> "*I think all people just assume kids are one way, and now after being in a class with George, they know that there are different types of kids with different problems and different needs.*"
>
> —George's mother

YOU CAN DO IT!

Remember that inclusive opportunities are your child's right. All parents have to work at ensuring the best possible experiences for their child, and your IFSP or IEP team can help you find preschool options that fit your family's and child's needs. Here are some guidelines:

- Don't be afraid to ask questions about the law, the lingo, or the system. Talk to professionals and other parents to get the information that you need, and use resources provided by family resource centers, parent support groups, and advocacy organizations.
- Create a file for all of your child's papers and your notes from meetings, and keep track of people with whom you have spoken and their responses to your questions.
- Be prepared for meetings. Have a list of issues or concerns that you want to discuss, and, if necessary, send reminder notes or make follow-up calls about meetings.
- State your goals and wishes for your child. You have the right to participate and be heard in the education process.
- Be aware of the goals, services, and strategies of your child's IEP. If you are not happy with a goal or service or are not sure that it is being carried out, say something.
- If you have difficulty bringing your child for therapy at a certain time or place, let your child's team know. Appropriate transportation and scheduling need to be made so that your child doesn't miss important appointments.
- Work with someone who is familiar with your culture and language.
- Develop relationships and connections with others in your community to exchange ideas and to ensure that your child has the support that she needs to grow and learn.

Other parents are also valuable sources of information and advice. Use the strategies and suggestions included in this booklet to get started, and work with other parents and professionals in your community. By working together, we can create positive preschool experiences for all children. Remember, you are the best advocate for your child!